ABOUT THE AUTHOR

Scarlett Ward is a Black Country poet working from Cannock, England. In 2019 she came runner up in Mother's Milk Poetry Prize, 3rd place in Wolverhampton Literature Prize, and runner up in the Verve Festival Community Poetry Competition. She was shortlisted for Best Spoken Word Poet by Saboteur Awards, and her work has featured in anthologies from Eye Flash Poetry, Hedgehog Press, and Fly On The Wall Poetry. Her micro-pamphlet *Rebirth* was published digitally with Irisi Press in 2016. She is a snail enthusiast and hopes to extend her family of giant land snails in due time.

Twitter: @scarlettwith2ts
www.facebook.com/Scarlett Ward
Instagram: @scarlett.ward

Scarlett Ward
ache

VERVE
POETRY PRESS
BIRMINGHAM

PUBLISHED BY VERVE POETRY PRESS
https://vervepoetrypress.com
mail@vervepoetrypress.com

FIRST PUBLISHED JUN 2019

Printed and bound in the UK
by Imprint Digital, Exeter

ISBN: 978-1-912565-23-8

For Jacob, you are the reason I stayed alive long enough to write any of this. You are, honestly and without any exaggeration, the reason I breathe at all. I love you.

CONTENTS

ii. To ache is to endure

iii. To ache is to love

iv. To ache is to recover

Scarlett's guest poets - Jess Davies, Sallyanne Rock and Rebecca Lockwood

Notes & Acknowledgements

ache

i. to ache is to heal

We're going to have to talk about it at some point

aren't we?
Except I don't want to.
Can't we talk instead of dandelion manes;
the way they nose their way through
cracks in the pavement,
only to be scattered in infinite directions
when kicked violently enough,
scorned spores spiraling;
frantic heads of fine-spun lace
dizzying themselves away,
as though away is the only place far enough
from that damned kicking boot.
Can we focus on the flowers
and not think of anything else -
not how I ran home to my mom's house,
shame dampening the crotch of my underwear,
and not the beads from my snapped bracelet
that I clutched tightly in my fist.

I don't know much about Catholicism

but for the sake of this poem say I do.
Say I'm the communion bread,
the thinly stretched wafer
molded into nipple-sized circles
that fit easily into the mouth
when placed on the tongue.

Say you place me on your tongue,
don't wait for me to soften before you chew.
Say I leave you feeling
absolved.

Say you do as you will with my body,
my soft girlish body,
all unrisen dough and uncooked,
as you do with the body of Christ;
pull it apart until it relents in your hands.
Say I am kneaded out by fist
and baked in stone fire,
chewed by your jaws,
torn apart by canine.

Say what you did was holy.
Say what you did was out of love.

Why then have you hidden me in your pocket
where you pray that God will never look?

In which the oyster refuses to open

then after *that,*
every word required a prising
apart of my reluctant jaw,
a sucking sound of a parting
seal, a pulling separate of
a gummy membrane
fastening, a cracking of
cockle-spine prying open
to get to the

Pearl.

I taste the metal of a blade
slipped in neatly
then twisted, feel
forceful widening of
mandibles.

> *"I'm doing alright, I promise."*

The clink of a sharp snap,
returning once more
to a tight
clasp.

I ask myself

After he touched you, you wanted to wrap yourself in black velvet / stand in a room with cardboard boxes glued to the ceiling to make your senses dead to all but that part. / You would have collected every stimulated nerve and kept it frozen in that state, / wouldn't you?
You would have trained them to dance for you the way they did then. / You would have needed a louder whistle. / You want to hold your arm in front of a mirror, / reflect the part of you he touched, back onto you again. / Isn't that a kind of cannibalism? You feel certain that you're eating yourself. / You are the only one that brings you sustenance anymore, / cloning that caress that nourished you/ but the result mutates further each time. / A river will meander from its course to leave its favourite rock untouched. You don't think you could allow anything else to touch you now. / You swear when the sun sets over an ocean it sets nowhere else, it's so focused on pouring itself into this one for you. / When they ask Where did he hurt you? You won't point to your heart, / you'll point to the spot on your neck where he ever so gently /
kissed you.

Purple
(Love Notes To My Depression.)

Let's lie so close together that we breathe in each other's
exhaled air over and over until we get dizzy from the carbon
dioxide and we won't be able to tell whose breath came first
and in that way we'll be tied together indelibly our faces will
become wet with condensation like an ordained christening
of holy water dripping from our brows because we won't ever
share vows or swap rings we'll share instead the molecules

of depleting oxygen passing them between us like bread
tearing off what we can and returning it again so many times
we'll forget it isn't sustainable so we'll exhale to match each
other until one of us chokes and I will think of how chimneys
belch great polluting clouds that purple the skies and how your
breath-starved lips look like waxy blackberries grown fat and
ripe for plucking.

Melanchole
(After Salvia Palth)

It is as though Melancholy has a landline,
and calls throughout the night,
as forceful in its persistence
as a newborn squeal for milk;
it is a chemical response ignited in the brain. Melancholy
won't accept answerphone, or when it does,
it leaves voicemail messages
of the heaviest silence you'll ever hear.
They can last days.
It never covers the charges.
It is as though Melancholy stored every number
ever written in lipstick on the back of toilet doors:
Call for a good time.
I guess Melancholy just loves the company.

Now its ring is a jingling question mark.
Drilling. Demanding.
It is those early hours that its sound has the sharpest edge,
and my ear drums begin a beckon roll that summons me
to this insistent, relentless phone.
Melancholy doesn't like being kept waiting.
It rings and rings,
and one day I know I'll have to disconnect the line,
but for now I just can't help myself
from cradling the mouthpiece to my lips,
and in a whisper as soft as nestling down
I answer;

I haven't forgotten you, love,
Let yourself in.

BPD

Remember that sometimes, when I talk,
it's not my voice that shouts,
It is that which takes over my mind
and makes my hands disappear.

It is not my voice that shouts
when an episode grips me
and makes the air dissolve my touch.
Just promise you'll hold me tightly

when an episode grips me,
And I float outwards from my skin.
Just promise to hold me tightly
And I'll try to find my way home.

And I float outwards from my skin -
It is that which takes over my mind.
And I'll try to find my way home.

Remember that, sometimes.

Spinner

I am a tall tale spinner,
braiding the fabric of myself;
surveying my silken thread of seconds
wound around each year of my life
passing it back and forth between my hands
trying to pull some sort of sense
from my loom of close encounters
and brief acquaintances -
Trying on their characteristics,
like an oversized second-hand coat.
With question marks for finger prints,
blank spaces underlined -
I'm still figuring out the dimensions
to the net of my identity
so that I can build it around myself
to see if I can fit inside,
and whether I can make it feel like home.
Because I don't recognise myself
outside the cloud of diagnoses,
or who I am beyond it.
I dig my fingernails under the edges of my disorder,
and pry it up like a dried paint lid,
to investigate what else there is to me.
So I tell myself tales of who I might be,
trying to judge the horizon
between performance
and being;
role, and the real me.

Although I don't know what I am,
I know that it's out there.
So I'll spin
and I'll spin
until I find something that fits.

X

I'm trying to smoke less.
That's why I only buy packs of
Ten now,
and not twenty.
Ten,
to keep my mouth busy
when I'm at a complete loss for words
because too many of them clamber at once for release.
Ten,
for when lashing out at other people
isn't working to fix what hurts,
so I smoke the air I should have used to tell you I was hurting.
Ten,
to fill my chest with soot
in the hopes that flowers will grow out of my mouth
like Technicolor gardens stuffed into my cavities.
Ten,
for diary pages folded away and never spoken of,
"I wish I wasn't so scared" scrawled in gel pen
tucked away into a cupboard drawer.
Ten
is just enough to scald my mouth
and burn away those words
I spat at my mother in hate.
Ten,
enough to keep my lungs inflated
when my heart drops heavy enough to collapse them
after seeing her crumple at words thrown at her
by a tongue her own body grew.

Ten,
for when I realized how easy it is to hurt someone
when that someone reminds you so much of yourself;
The only Mother tongue I inherited is my mother's inability to use it.
Ten,
for times when all I want to do
is just to scream my apologies,
but my mouth is a cave of velvet that swallows my words.
It's only sometimes,
I need those
Ten.
I'm trying to smoke less.

I grew

- With soil tucked into unwashed cuticles.
With fingers planted like ginger roots
in the unruly garden of the house I learned to walk in.

- Gradually, and measured in
a grass blade's width,
never in mighty trunk rings.

- By uprooting the chalky skull of a long silent robin;
the squeak of shovel against bone proof
that maybe even dead birds still sing.

- Wondering what God would think of my implosion
after he hauled me into this world
from something smaller than grain
(or indeed my mother after she did the same).

The smiling yellow pistil

Mother the apple bough,
bowed herself with bearing.
Mother the fracture in bent bark,
and frost-frozen soil
on tenderstem roots.

Mother the daisy
who plucked at her mane
twice each time around
so that I never landed on
"they love me not."

Mother the bald yellow centre;
the smiling yellow pistil.

Mother the shower of Autumn fronds,
the silken dew droplets she wept;
the confetti shuddered free of herself
gladly given to the earth like fanfare.

Mother the kindling,
and, too, the labourer,
that whittled and hacked
away at parts of herself

so that I might never go without.

Sunflower

I buried your beetle-back
casing in the compost

and read sonnets to
your rooted sapling spine.

We waited together
- alone, just us -

for strength to seep
through your stalk veins,

drawn from the vibrations
rippled from my voice;

There is something
to be celebrated about

the shuddered sun-turned sun
of your heliotropic head,

the boast of canary plumage,
and the pride in both our faces

when, against all odds, you bloomed,
and I didn't kill myself.

Kitchen windows

After accidentally pulling the hardened handle of a mop
swiftly into her chest whilst cleaning the kitchen window,
and cracking the two ribs that greeted the chiselled wood
into the cavity of breath that was her body, my mother told me

There's some broken bones you just can't get at to bind

and carried on with her chores, although all the skin from her breast
to her navel was blackened, as though she bore
violent storm clouds under her flesh.

(The last time her ribs ached like this
they guarded the whisper
of my own heartbeat.
How we forget what a clenched-fist thump
the shrug of a pulse can be.)

Only when I got older would I understand what it was
to have your body break from the inside out
and seal the fractures yourself;
that is to say it took me years to gather the strength
to haul my illness around after me
like a wind-torn branch warping the posture of an oak,
instead of trying to cut it out
with the sharpened end of
lonely.

My mother's ribs healed.
We still collect acorns together sometimes.

Recovery

In small sips, remind your body what it is to be nourished.
Drink tea; milky, sugared.
Force a dust-covered wall-switch to click on light.
Sing along to the tap water hitting a bone-dry sink.
Imagine everything blooming as you swallow it;
like Indian ink, or watercolour,
or the blooded gums of a fire eater,
lighting up corners of your stomach,
corneas of your eyes,
and the liquid pool inside your ears.
Remind yourself that you are more than just a cave,
or anything else that is measured by its emptiness.
Make room for something other than the nothing.
Be careful, sip slowly so as not to bloat.
The knots you unpack will leave rope burns on your hands.
Remember how you had once become a sailor's net?
Your body will leak salt as though anointing itself
in the waves of its own sea. You are done drowning.
Each spoon is a cargo ship.
Each plate is a harbour.
We all pray for safe passage this time.
The cutlery will applaud as you pull open the drawer.
The captain bows. You eat.

What I chose to spend my birthday money on rather than a prescription for antidepressants

A tin of yellow paint.
The Dulux colour chart called it
Sunflower Sunshine.

I covered my bedroom wall with the dates
of every day I thought about dying,

And I decorated the numbers with flowers to remind myself
I never did.

ii. to ache is to endure

Culling season

Somewhere in a town that is best known
for how deep it has dug beneath itself,
where the addresses are earthy like "May Dene" and "Old Fallow",
and roads fling themselves lethargically around woodland bends,
a pot hole rips the gut out of an exhaust on an accelerating Ford
with all the viciousness of antlers on bark. After all, it is rutting season,
and it's all I can think of lately; feuding stags butting skulls,
concrete tearing out metal piping,
and the way my neighbour boasted to me this morning
of the fawn he shot through the eye socket.

Snow

I feel your pelvis sink into my pelvis and my pelvis sink into the mattress and I have spent so many weeks sharpening my hip bones I never realised that the sharper they got the more they would become fence posts keeping you at your distance even when you were inside of me. You empty into my body like melting snow but I remain glacial; unmoved and cold. You don't notice.

So now it's just you and I and this room - except it's not - it is this room, and you and I are happening to it rather than to each other. I said I hate it when you said my name because you always make it sound like a question, and nothing you ever say sounds quite certain.

Your love cost more than the rolled-up notes shoved into your pocket; you taught me to crush up my affection. You numbed my mouth and every other part of me you touched. I soon learned that if you've got to hold one nostril while you're inhaling to breathe easy then darling that's not respiration that's recreation and that shit will kill you; but just never as fast as you'd like.

I wish you would stop bleeding from the palms of your hands long enough to realise you're not actually a martyr you're only playing the role, and I am done with applauding until my palms are sore - can't you see the irony?

I can no longer beg for you to make room in your mouth for more *"I love you"*s when I have cracked my teeth biting my tongue to stop the words from spilling out too often. The marrow lakes within my bones are parched, salty and powdered, and not entirely unlike snow.

High

The bleached reptile-scale of roof tiles -
The cracked white knuckle of a pigeon on wing -
The misted frosty droplets in the gap

between the glazed glass panes of an airplane window -
The moment it occurs to cloud to turn rain into sleet -
The soft amniotic pearl of ozone that cradles us -

The transmission of a voice flung out across airwaves,
along wires than span miles like vocal chords
and up to the satellites that stalk us -

and indeed whatever else might be above that.
Only when I was soaring in the palm of the nameless
Deity that carries us, could I,

bloody-nosed,
dopamine-drunk,
and sense all but obliterated,

tolerate any of it,
any of myself,
any of anything.

Crockery spines

There is a chipped bowl
in the cupboard,
with five more
stacked on top of it.

Its embrace is full
with the domed spinal column of another
cradled against its hollowed belly,

but technically.
it is still

                                        empty.

Every piece is titled *"Home"*

and the galleries are angry at me
for filling their walls hanging prints
from the bottom of your trainers.
I have filled great glass tanks with earth
dug from beneath your bus stop
and filled vials with rain from your gutter.
Wet bath towels droop from the ceiling,
suspended by wire, like they are
national emblems, or great surrender flags.

A projector throws x-rays of your dental records
against a crumpled king-sized bedsheet,
and your answer machine message is set on repeat,
played over a Tannoy of broken speakers
so that the only words that stutter out are
"here ... leave ... get back to you."
I have licked the back of every shopping receipt
and palm-smacked the paper to plaster
until I have created a map of our old house.

I don't have an artist's biography,
but there is a cellar downstairs
that is flooded with my sweat,
or maybe it's tears.
Shall we go swimming?
and you can tell me which point of my life
you believe all this salt came from,
or how much of yourself
you can taste when you drink it.

I can't help myself

A finger pressed on the purple of a
bruise and reopened birthday
cards. A tongue stuck into a loose
filling and re read text

messages. Scorched sore
sinuses and hoarded aftershave
bottles. The frayed tag of a
cuticle and a worn campus

jumper. A nail imposed on the head
of a scab and a name repeated into a
mirror. Fingers bent
to cracking point and a practiced

signature. Knife teeth pressed
onto a thumb and forgotten wax
records. A breath held until
it's uncomfortable. I

can't help it. I still can't
get over you.

How I can bear to drive past your address

1.   I talk about the M6 as though it exists in past tense; A relic of a bygone era that archaeologists will dig up when they study what heartbreak looked like in the 21st century; The long spine of a creature that left its vertebrae in the potholes between the arc-backed junctions 9 and 6.

2.   I siphon out the petrol it takes me to get to Birmingham and use it to drown the cacti you bought me so that I can't drive past your window and wonder if you've left it open like you always did, and whether you're warm enough.

3.   I pretend your city is now in ruins, and ivy has pulled apart the foundations like a loaf relenting in the hands of Christ. The name of the street you live on now sounds like Latin, or some other dead language, like a verse from the old testament, like the garden of Eden; a pasture, lost.

4.   I tell myself that if Rome is named so because Romulus killed Remus then we should name this city Disappointment, and my Love was the wolf-breast from which it suckled 'til it had strength enough to destroy everything we built, that *Rome wasn't built it a day*. It took us two years - and only a fraction of that to demolish.

One hundred and six miles

When I'm there, I wake up under a different sky.
A white lighthouse scalpels its screaming beam
across the inky velvet night.
A million stars bite into its cold crisp surface
leaving teeth marks which twinkle,
and hemorrhage carbon
and little girls' wishes.
Every sigh of the surf baptizes the shells
which emboss the glass-clear body of ocean.
Is water cleansing, or erasing?
I'm not so sure I can tell the difference anymore.

Meanwhile, my heritage is pebble-dashed charcoal grit;
It's rusted copper veins,
hunted into the womb of the earth;
an umbilicus of precious coal to
a placenta of fossil nourishment;
pursued by pick axe and chisel
by our leather-faced, achy lunged grandfathers.
Our mother tongue curls around exaggerated vowels -
soft, like the breast of a wet nurse
and we wean that softness into our voices
'till they are Pendulous and rhythmic,
even when warning children of violent sinkholes
that drop way suddenly between the thick cloak of Fir trees.

It is one hundred and six miles from familiar soot-drenched air,
man-planted clockwork forests, and puddles that accrue like dinner
        table ashtrays,

that a cold breeze whisks up a western tide
a lost seagull wails on the wind,
and I am so very far from home.

Tide times

02:54

The pier settled into the full basin of the docks. The harbour filled as it hoarded the water jealously, stowing away the slap of its full stomach in one great gulp. Waves always grow slow when fat. The ocean was a slicked black onyx bead in the moonlight.

10:23

Barnacle-white
freckles flaked
from boats' underbellies
like a brittle
carcass
of bloated whale
stomach.
My mouth, bone dry.

15:39

There was just sand enough for two bodies and a side-by-side stroll. I remembered hearing of gritty particles discovered sticking to Monet paintings and imagined small atoms of the beach attaching themselves to me. I dug my hands deep into the sand and welcomed dirty nails. I wanted to carry as much of this place with me as I could. I wanted to be his Monet painting. Had anyone put me under a microscope they'd be able to record every kiss he left on my palm. I could count them on one hand.

23:08
A long finger of land
grasped for the shore
at the opposite end of the cove.
He broke gate with me
to pick up
a cockle shell.
I kept it in my pocket,

And discovered it three weeks later,
when sat at my office desk.

The language of flowers

i.   Dahlias
That year is a gravestone.
My only memories stand petrified
like churchyard gargoyles
and neglected tombs;
unvisited, abandoned.

ii.   Peonies
I do not bring bouquets, or
mourn passing, do not revisit stories
or read cracked epitaphs.
I let your phantom shadow that place and
I do not visit. I chant to keep me from your spectre.
Stay dead, stay dead, stay dead.

iii.   Orange lilies
That year is a faceless cast.
Mannequins with polished heads.
Names are buried six feet deep.
Ghosts.

iv.   Rhododendrons
Entire crypts are overgrown
with carnations and marigolds.
The brighter the blood, the fresher the wound.
The crooked spines of elm trees twist to cast shade.

v.   *Carnations*
I'm afraid if I speak your name
it will summon you before me,
so I throw salt over my doors to keep you at bay.
Mostly, it's working.
Mostly.

vi.   *Daffodils*
I'd rather a single year chiselled
into a gravestone, and let it rot in peace
than my own name -
which was so nearly the case.

iii. to ache is to adore

What is true of Spring

is true also of ourselves.

Learn from her;
how she unfurls her flowered fists,

      waits for buds to burst from the end of branches,
            like beading blood on kneecaps,
                  or lacquer slicked at the end of knuckled hands.

Heal from your wounds womb first; blood
               is no omen of Death, but of the pact we make
     with Life.

                    Even fossils dream of dawn,
           brittle from singing themselves hoarse
             clinking away under all that soil
             like forgotten coins in a deep pocket
                waiting to be unearthed.

              What if none of us ever stopped singing,
       the same way an Oak remembers its notes of green
                once April comes back around
     no matter how much white Winter had buried it in?

How I fell in love

Not like a harvest leaf,
shuddered loose by branches
to bare their bird-nest hearts,

Neither graceful nor silent
as snow from cushioned clouds
in light pursuit of blanketed drifts,

Nor like the soft feather
from its fan of spines,
coaxed by the wind's draw.

No, but see instead
how completely I gave myself
to gravity. How completely.

Your name

It is incomprehensible now to think
that my tongue once did not break its back

to curl around your name
the way it does now; the letters previously just

signposts for specific sounds,
but now my mouth creases a certain way

like an overspent pound note,
never able to sit flat the same again.

It is incomprehensible
that before those letters aligned

like constellations, mapping you onto my sky,
that name was just a sound,

like any other kind of music is just sound
until you've heard it enough to recognize it,

and then it becomes a song,
your favourite song. You are my favourite

song to sing. You are
my favourite tongue twister

I have ever managed to master, you stick
between my teeth like pomegranate pips

and I spit and I spit, but I
can't get rid of the taste. It is

incomprehensible to think that I can use words
that I used before you, about

anything else other than you,
without them being drenched

in you. It is incomprehensible that there is
anyone else out there with your name

because every letter in it
belongs only to you.

Strawberry

I bet
the day you were born
I was eating strawberries for the first time,

smashing soft fruit flesh into my rosebud mouth,
smearing syrupy juice across my blushed cheek
with the back of a fat dimpled hand,
and cackling indulgently at my exquisite discovery.

I bet
the day you were born
I was having the sweetest day of my short life.

Clinging

There is a certain corner of the world
that has only ever existed throughout history
so that you might happen to it.

There is a field, and a pub, and a canal
and alongside it grows grass,
and among it, a single dewy wisp
that knew all along

before it burst from its anther pod,
root stretched into earth bed soil,
while still cosy in the womb of its blade
and not yet fledged by wind nor bird,

that it would end its life
bent in the tread of your shoe
like a bowed Monk's back in prayer;

and still it busied itself in growing
so that it might get trodden on
in just the right way, by you
at just the right time, by you.

I keep your boots by the doorway, love.
I too know what it is to live clinging to your every step.

Autumn

What you don't know
is that today
I walked through the city for hours
trying to find a leaf
with the exact same shade as your eyes

- saccharine shades of
zucchini with an unripe
tangerine tinge,
a stolen second of spilt
watercolour on drab
granite slate -

just so I could call you
and let you know
that I found a leaf
with the exact same shade as your eyes.

Seen

I don't know
How he does it,
But he looks at me
Like it's the first time
That he's ever seen me,
And at the same time
Like it would be
The very last.

A sonnet to every Love that came before me

If, when you lay with your head on his chest,
you couldn't hear a century's worth of music in each breath,
and couldn't feel every perfect thing in this world
condensed, distilled, concentrated,
into that simple inwards/outwards motion -

And if there was a single ounce of you
that wasn't pressed to the very vibrations of his pulse
tapping against your flattened eardrum
like a child's fingertip against aquarium glass,
like the downy underwing of an owl through the air,

Or if it didn't strike you how like Morse
it was, hammering out the directions
to every dream you'd brain-whisked into wish,
but never thought you'd find in existence,

Then either you weren't listening hard enough
or, put plainly, you simply didn't deserve him.

We have our own language

Centre Of Palms,
Bottom Of Soles,

We talk in
Inside Of Kneecaps.

We are fluent in these tongues.
We are scholars of each other's.

You whisper *"come here"*
in the speech of *Eye Contact.*

It reverberates from the socket.

And *Here* is a coordinate of air
right in front of your face, and I fill it

with myself
so that there is no *There* or

any of the distance it brings -
no word for it in our dictionary.

There is no room,
because in all of our languages,

all the words for *Here*
fill the space between our mouths

that were so used to feeling so empty.

In this version of reality I never found you

In this version it's still *sunrise/ day/ breathe/ sunset/ night,*
but its without you, so perhaps its less *breathe* and more

sunset/ night/ sunset/ night/ sunset/ night.
In this reality there's just enough memory of a sun

to acknowledge that it's setting, but without
it ever having quite risen in the first place,

as though I exist in an eternal cycle of
dusk/sunset/night/dusk/sunset/night.

There's enough twilight to suggest something is setting;
We recall there must have been a sunrise at some point,

and I am still looking for it,
or at least enough of it in another person

that I can fool myself into thinking it's the same thing.
I should know better by now, but in this alternate reality I don't.

So I start every day *wakeup/cold/sunset/wake up/cold/sunset*
the memory of a sun rattling around in a crinkle of my brain.

like a forgotten pebble made absurd
by the alien environment you found it in;

A coin in a discarded coat lining/
A seashell in a car door.

In this version of reality,
I never found you,

And all of it is just an eternal
dark/dark/

/dark.

One bedroom

We have taken the stars into our mouths,
Gulped great corners of the galaxy
So that when we grin we glare with all the brightness
Of dying suns behind our teeth.
And that's just it, isn't it; to love is to ache
And to ache is to hunger,
So in hunger we consume what we can of the universe,
Taking in as much as we can fit inside ourselves
So that it never leaves,
Filling out hollowed-out stomachs with space and light
And one another
So we can hibernate in what we have gathered,
Piling our bites of sky on top of one another
Like a nest that we turn around and around in
Like dogs, in the den we have carved out -
How delicious it is to love a corner of the world
As though it has never belonged to anybody else,
As though we too deserve the same exoneration;
To be the precious star someone has discovered and
Exclaimed, *"Yes! Want!"*
And put their name to it.

Buttercup

Waxy mustard saucers, they are
spilling shades of citrine as they pour -
reflecting it onto peach-down skin
when thrust under my chin.
My face is jutted day-ward and
the glowing orb at my throat confirms, yes,

    I love, my love,
        I love.

But if I lift my left hand
to your lips and under your gaze,
will it turn yours yellow too
when you announce to me *"I do"*
like a lime litmus of truth?
The buds grow, anxious-
These acres of stemmed proposals,
these fields of cracked yolks;
They all ask

    Do you love, my love?
        Do you love?

If I rip enough fist-fulls
out from their quilted earth beds,
and gather them all to your face,
will they shine all the brighter,

as little ochre oracles
when you promise to me
every one of your tomorrows?
Will you love, my love?
Will you always love?

iv. to ache is to recover

To ache is to

bleed, to clot, to suck at a wound and
know that to ingest your own blood is a part of
what it means to heal. To ache is to learn that
sometimes swallowing Wolfsbane and steeling your
organs by howling at the full moon is a better choice
than spitting the root out and never knowing the madness of
running with a pack. To ache is to know that pain isn't
an absence of love, but rather the exit wound where
it fell from the raw softness of your body -
and in the face of all that hurt, you heal again anyway,
with a ribcage made all the stronger for Love to roost
and nestle between your lungs,
and be cradled by everything that you are,
when Summer comes back around.

end

Scarlett Introduces...

Jess Davies

As mentioned in my acknowledgements, Jess was the very first person to extend her friendship to this little out-of-town loner with when I debuted on the Birmingham poetry scene, which I will always be grateful for. Her kindness is matched only by her talent. Every time she performs I am left open-mouthed and breathless. Jess' words will sucker-punch you in the gut, but then nurse you better again with their tenderness. Her poetry's deep understanding and exploration of the vulnerabilities of all that it is to be human makes her work so powerfully moving. I am beyond honored to have her feature.

Jess is founder of regular poetry night "Stirchley Speaks", which opens its doors to open mic'ers and guest supports. I saw her support American viral poet Neil Hilborn at The Glee Club in Birmingham and have adored her poetry ever since.

Dissecting flowers

Pierce stem with nail -
>   create green rub with finger and thumb,
>   allow it to stain the keratin.

Suspend the roots -
>   investigate where they came from.

Hold out its' life form at eye level -
>   give it a view of the landscape,
>   frame the earth with sky.

When you bring it back -
>   pulp the leaves and pull apart what you don't understand.

Knot soft blades until they stop stinging -
>   throw petals like reunion, anniversary and wedding.

Sing a eulogy for the sacrifice every morning and night -
>   Implant the notes in your bones,
>   carry the seeds home.

Draw them out tender, in graphite reference;
>   'A Phoenix botanical work'

Hope the depiction smells like charcoal -
>   a portrait of reincarnation.

Sallyanne Rock

Since shedding her pen name alias and evolving further into the
brave and skilled poet that she is, I have simply fallen
further and further in love with Sally, to the point we now refer
to each other as "poetry sisters." I kept bumping into Sally at
poetry events and seeing her name pop up in poetry
magazines, which is testament not only to her hard work and
determination, but also to her wide and ever-increasing
accomplishments. I am so grateful she agreed to feature a poem
in my collection.

Sallyanne Rock is a poet and writer living in Worcestershire.
Her work appears in various journals online and in print, and
she has performed her poetry across the Midlands region. She
is currently working with Writing West Midlands as an
Assistant Writer, running a series of creative writing workshops
for young people.

On the bypass

I drove around the curve of you
when you were newly still
and sleep-like

imagined your eye shine
low slink
of umber pelt

every day I passed
with the heaviness
of your rain-drenched fur

blackening on the asphalt
that could not welcome you
back into the earth

after three weeks
gathering grit and cigarette-ends
they swept and sluiced
dropped a traffic cone gravestone

you   in an industrial bin bag
and me   not ready to let go

Rebecca Lockwood

I owe so much to poetry and all that I have got from it, but I have to say the best thing it brought me was my friendship with Bec. Although we only lived down the road from each other all our lives, we only met through poetry nights a few years ago, and since then I am so blessed to get to call her one of my best friends. I remember hearing her perform for the first time and it ripped my heart out, so it came as no surprise when she won the position of young Poet Laureate of Staffordshire and released her own collection *Grace* with Fishbowl Publishing. I truly believe that there is something about poetry that forces you to bare all the raw parts of your soul, and that opens you up to form incredibly strong bonds such as this. I'm so thankful Becca agreed to showcase her poem here.

Supper

We were out for dinner
We left together.
Slipping through the
Streets
So blatantly estranged.

The branches of leaves on the
Trees, committed to the pathway,
Seemed to slip like snakes around
Our necks
Forbidding our ability to
Talk
To one another.

We sat and that was all.
The Italian singer, a lucky distraction
From the void in the centre of the table
That nobody had broken the bread
And the wine left was beginning to
Look like the blood of lambs.
The waiter morphed into anything
We could force into small talk.
We paid the bill
We left together
On the route back
All I could hear was the
Crush of my shoes on the pavement
The wail of the wind

In the Trees
The brush of your
Bag on your side
This new erray of silent
Sounds made it too easy
For me to see
Your pace speed up
So you did not have
To walk next to me

And from all of this
All I have learnt
Is how lucky you are
If the only time
You feel lonely
Is when you are
Alone.

ACKNOWLEDGEMENTS

Firstly to my sister Darcy, the biggest mistake I have ever made was ever thinking I was alone. Thank you for always being there for me. I love you forever.

To my mom and dad, thank you for the support, for pushing me, and never giving up on me. I love you all the way to the milky way and back (and that's a long way!)

To Stuart, for believing in my potential, and for encouraging me to take my time to develop my own voice before publishing me. I needed that year or so to find myself and without it I don't think this book would have taken shape the way it has. Being able to release a book with Verve Poetry Press and getting to work with the amazing people behind it has been a total dream.

A huge thank you to Liz Berry, whose voice inspired me to write in my own way, and without any shame of my accent. I am so grateful for your friendship, help and encouragement, thank you.

To my university lecturer, Joe Stretch, who in my first year told me that my prose was "too flowery" and suggested "maybe try poetry".

I also want to thank with all my heart Chloe Frayne, whose friendship I value so dearly. Thank you for the quote review you wrote for my cover and for the gentle and unwavering support. You are a ray of sunshine.

To Ashley Luka, my rock. For all the days you drove to my house just to sit with me while I cried. For all the fun adventures. For everything you've ever done for me, thank you. I love you!

To my poetry 'big sister' Sallyanne, you are an absolute inspiration. Your friendship has guided me through some difficult moments and I am so grateful for the strength you have given me.

Thank you to Roy McFarlane for selecting my poem *We're going to have to talk about it at some point* as 3rd place winner at the WOLF competition, and for the organisers of Wolverhampton Literature

Thank you to Leon Priestnall, who included my work in the back of his book and who gave me the opportunity to perform at Howl poetry nights when I was still very new to the poetry scene.

To Jess Davies, who befriended me at my first Birmingham gig when I was stood alone in the line. I'm still as star struck to know you now as I was back then.

I'm also very grateful to Isabelle Kenyon, who helped me copy check my words when this collection was in its infancy and posted back a version with love hearts drawn on for encouragement. Thanks too go to Fly On The Wall Press, who first published the poem *Spinner* in the charity anthology *Persona Non Grata*.

To anyone I hurt, I'm sorry. To anyone that hurt me, thank you - it's because of you that I grew.

ABOUT VERVE POETRY PRESS

Verve Poetry Festival is a new press focussing intently on meeting a local need in Birmingham - a need for the vibrant poetry scene here in Brum to find a way to present itself to the poetry world via publication. Co-founded by Stuart Bartholomew and Amerah Saleh, it is publishing poets from all corners of the city - poets that represent the city's varied and energetic qualities and will communicate its many poetic stories.

Added to this is a colourful pamphlet series featuring poets who have previously performed at our sister festival - and a poetry show series which captures the magic of longer poetry performance pieces by poets such as Polarbear and Matt Abbott.

Like the festival, we will strive to think about poetry in inclusive ways and embrace the multiplicity of approaches towards this glorious art.

www.vervepoetrypress.com
@VervePoetryPres
mail@vervepoetrypress.com